MCR

Spy Kid

FAMOUS SPIES

Deanna Caswell

BLACK RABBIT BOOKS

Hi Jinx is published by Black Rabbit Books
P.O. Box 3263, Mankato, Minnesota, 56002.
www.blackrabbitbooks.com
Copyright © 2019 Black Rabbit Books

Marysa Storm, editor; Michael Sellner, designer;
Grant Gould, production designer;
Omay Ayres, photo researcher

Library of Congress Cataloging-in-Publication Data
Names: Caswell, Deanna, author.
Title: Famous Spies / by Deanna Caswell.
Description: Mankato, Minnesota : Black Rabbit Books,
2019. | Series: Hi Jinx. Spy Kid | Includes bibliographical
references and index.
Identifiers: LCCN 2017051482 (print) | LCCN 2018004962
(ebook) | ISBN 9781680725919 (e-book) | ISBN
9781680725858 (library binding) | ISBN 9781680727395
(paperback)
Subjects: LCSH: Spies–Juvenile literature. | Espionage–Juvenile
literature.
Classification: LCC UB270.5 (ebook) | LCC UB270.5 .C37 2018
(print) | DDC 327.12092/2–dc23
LC record available at https://lccn.loc.gov/2017051482

Printed in the United States. 4/18

Image Credits

CONTENTS

4

Chapter 1
TOP SECRET

A spy drives down a back road to the drop site. Once he arrives, he finds the **dead drop**. This time, the enemy spies left their messages in an empty pear can.

The spy takes the can and leaves behind several canisters. They're filled with secret U.S. documents. The man isn't actually betraying his country, though. He's setting a trap. When the enemy spies arrive, the FBI will catch them with the secrets.

Undercover

Spies are popular in books and movies. But spies go on missions in real life too. They gather information for their governments. Many enter enemy territory. They might pretend to be someone else. Very few people know what spies do. It's only after missions are long done that most stories come out.

Sidney Reily

James Bond

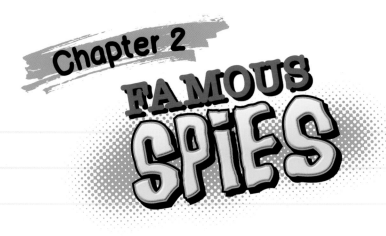

Chapter 2
FAMOUS SPIES

Several spies **inspired** the character James Bond. Sidney Reilly was one of them. Reilly spied for Great Britain. He spoke many languages. He was also a master of disguise. During one mission, he dressed as a **priest**. On another, he pretended to be a shipyard worker. His disguise helped him steal information about a German factory.

One story says Reilly fought off cannibals in a jungle.

Courageous and Confident

Krystyna Skarbek spied for Britain during World War II. She was calm and confident. Skarbek helped many **refugees** to safety. She rescued fellow agents from capture. Enemies captured Skarbek several times. But she always managed to escape. Once, while being questioned, Skarbek bit her tongue and coughed up blood. Afraid she was sick, the soldiers let her go.

Hall did all of her spying with a fake leg. She lost her real leg in a hunting accident.

The Limping Lady

Virginia Hall spied for Britain and the United States during World War II. Hall was adventurous and a great actor. While pretending to be a reporter, she **recruited** spies. She also gathered information about enemy Germans.

Hall then disguised herself as an old farm woman. She sent secret messages to resistance groups. She also trained fighters to **sabotage** the Germans. They slowed down the Germans by destroying bridges. They also derailed trains.

Enemy soldiers tried to capture Hall. But they never did.

Accidental Spy

During World War II, the British government asked for pictures of the French coast. Wanting to help, Odette Hallowes sent some in. The photos impressed the government. They asked Hallowes to be a spy.

Hallowes never meant to be a spy. But she was a great one. She worked as a radio operator in enemy territory. Another spy betrayed Hallowes, though. The enemy captured and tortured her. But she never once spilled her secrets.

radio operator

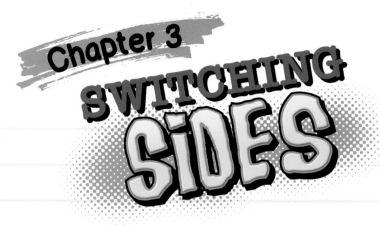

Chapter 3
SWITCHING SIDES

Spies sometimes work against their countries. Some spies do it because they don't like their governments. Others simply want money.

Adolf Tolkachev was an airplane specialist for the **Soviet Union**. He worked with **stealth** technology in the mid- to late-1900s. Tolkachev wasn't happy with his government, though. He photographed thousands of secret documents. His actions put his life at risk. But that did not stop him. Tolkachev shared the pictures with U.S. CIA agents for almost 10 years.

Double Agent

Aldrich Ames worked for the CIA. He wanted more money than he was making, though. He decided to sell secrets to the Soviet Union. For nine years, he traded information for money. He shared information about other spies. He blew many **double agents'** covers, including Tolkachev's. Ames even betrayed one of his friends.

Eventually, CIA members caught Ames. They arrested him in 1994.

Ames made more than $1 million selling secrets.

Chapter 4
GET IN ON THE Hi JiNX

Governments still use spies today. Only a few people know who they really are.

U.S. spies are part of the CIA. People wanting to become CIA agents must know **foreign** languages. They need experience living or traveling in other countries. They need good people skills too. And that's just the beginning!

Take It One Step More

1. Spies use disguises to find out information. Do you think it's OK to trick people to gather information? Why or why not?

2. Some spies work against their countries. Why would they do that?

3. What traits do most spies seem to have in common?

GLOSSARY

cannibal (KAN-uh-buhl)—a person who eats the flesh of human beings or an animal that eats its own kind

dead drop (DED DROP)—a prearranged hiding place for the placement and pickup of information

double agent (DUH-buhl EY-juhnt)—a spy who pretends to work for one government while actually spying for another

foreign (FAWR-in)—in a place or country other than the one a person is from

inspire (in-SPIHR)—to make someone want to do something

priest (PREEST)—a person who has the authority to lead or perform religious ceremonies

recruit (ri-KROOT)—to find suitable people and get them to join a company, an organization, or the armed forces

refugee (ref-yoo-JEE)—a person who flees his or her country for safety usually because of war or for religious reasons

sabotage (SAB-uh-tahzh)—to destroy or damage something on purpose so it does not work correctly

Soviet Union (SOH-ve-uht YOON-yun)—a former country in eastern Europe and northern Asia

stealth (STELTH)—an aircraft design that is hard for radar to pick up

BOOKS

Caswell, Deanna. *Famous Spy Missions.* Spy Kid. Mankato, MN: Black Rabbit Books, 2019.

Kallen, Stuart A. *World War II Spies and Secret Agents.* Heroes of World War II. Minneapolis: Lerner Publications, 2018.

Larson, Kirsten W. *The CIA.* Protecting Our People. Mankato, MN: Amicus High Interest, 2017.

WEBSITES

FBI — Kids
archives.fbi.gov/archives/fun-games/kids

KidSpy Zone
www.spymuseum.org/education-programs/kids-families/kidspy-zone/

Kids' Zone
https://www.cia.gov/kids-page

INDEX